D1363228

SUNNY SIDE PLUCKED

Rita Ann Higgins

SUNNY SIDE PLUCKED

NEW & SELECTED POEMS

BLOODAXE BOOKS

Copyright © Rita Ann Higgins 1986, 1988, 1992, 1996

ISBN: 1 85224 375 9

First published 1996 by
Bloodaxe Books Ltd,
P.O. Box 1SN,
Newcastle upon Tyne NE99 1SN.

Bloodaxe Books Ltd acknowledges
the financial assistance of Northern Arts.

LEGAL NOTICE

All rights reserved. No part of this book may be
reproduced, stored in a retrieval system, or
transmitted in any form, or by any means, electronic,
mechanical, photocopying, recording or otherwise,
without prior written permission from Bloodaxe Books Ltd.

Requests to publish work from this book
must be sent to Bloodaxe Books Ltd.

Rita Ann Higgins has asserted her right under
Section 77 of the Copyright, Designs and Patents Act 1988
to be identified as the author of this work.

Cover printing by J. Thomson Colour Printers Ltd, Glasgow.

Printed in Great Britain by
Cromwell Press Ltd, Broughton Gifford, Melksham, Wiltshire.

FOR MY SISTERS AND BROTHERS
Mary, Bernadette, Carmel, Alice,
Anthony, John, Joe, Gerry, Bartley,
Máirtín, Dominic and Brendan

Acknowledgements

This book includes poems selected from Rita Ann Higgins's collections *Goddess on the Mervue Bus* (1986), *Witch in the Bushes* (1988), *Philomena's Revenge* (1992) and *Higher Purchase* (1996), all published by Salmon Publishing. Those four books include many more poems, and copies are still available from Salmon Publishing Ltd, Knockeven, Cliffs of Moher, Co. Clare, Ireland.

Contents

FROM **GODDESS ON THE MERVUE BUS** (1986)

12 Consumptive in the Library
13 Evangeline
15 Mrs McEttigan
16 Tommy's Wife
17 Unnecessary Work
18 Work On
19 The Apprentices
20 Power Cut
21 Poetry Doesn't Pay
23 Goddess on the Mervue Bus
24 The German for Stomach
26 Almost Communication
27 Middle-aged Irish Mothers
29 Ode to Rahoon Flats
30 The Long Ward
32 God-of-the-Hatch Man
34 Mona
36 Sunny Side Plucked

FROM **WITCH IN THE BUSHES** (1988)

38 It's All Because We're Working-Class
40 She Is Not Afraid of Burglars
41 It Wasn't the Father's Fault
42 The Did-You-Come-Yets of the Western World
44 Be Someone
45 Old Soldier
46 Witch in the Bushes
49 Anything Is Better than Emptying Bins
51 Second Thoughts
55 He Fought Pigeons' Arses, Didn't He?
56 I Went to School with You
58 End of a Free Ride
59 The Tell Tattler
61 Woman's Inhumanity to Woman
63 The Blanket Man
64 No Balls at All
66 Peter Picasso
68 Some People

FROM **PHILOMENA'S REVENGE** (1992)

70   They Believe in Clint Eastwood
71   God Dodgers Anonymous
73   Every Second Sunday
74   Him and His Terrier
75   Reading
77   Philomena's Revenge
79   People Who Wear Cardigans Are Subversive
82   Misogynist
83   The Deserter
85   Questionaire After Leaving Ailwee Cave
87   Light of the Moon
89   Cloud talker
91   Old Timers
93   His Shoulder Blades and Rome
94   Butter Balls
96   Dead Dogs and Nations
98   I'll Have to Stop Thinking About Sex
100   Between Them
102   He Leaves the Ironing Board Open
103   Space Invader
105   Limits
107   Rat-Like Dogs and Tattooed Men
109   It's Platonic
110   If You Want to Get Closer to God
112   New York
113   H-Block Shuttle
116   Trapped Doctor on Cork to Galway Bus
118   The Power of Prayer
120   Jackdaw Jaundice
121   I Want to Make Love to Kim Basinger

FROM **HIGHER PURCHASE** (1996)

126   The Flogger
128   He Could Get Radio Prague
129   He Is Not Thinking About Last Night
132   Donna Laura
134   Higher Purchase
135   When the Big Boys Pulled Out
137   The Flute Girl's Dialogue
139   The Trouble with Karen Reilly

140   Mothercare
141   The Quarrel
143   Whiplashed
145   Remapping the Borders
146   Mamorexia
147   The Winner
149   The Taxi Man Knows
150   When It Comes to the Crutch
156   Gretta's Hex
154   Prism
155   The Temptations of Phillida
156   Spiked
158   Night Noon and Nora

FROM **GODDESS
ON THE MERVUE BUS**

(1986)

Consumptive in the Library

About you:
you carry a kidney donor card,
not yet filled in,
a St Christopher's round your neck
on a brown shoe lace,
(to ward off demons and politicians),
memories of Sweet Afton,
the racing page from the *Daily Express*
and an unsociable cough.

About me:
I carry illusions
of becoming a famous poet,
guilt about that one time in Baltinglass,
fear that the lift will stop at Limbo,
a slight touch of sciatica
plus an anthology of the Ulster poets.

Unlike your peers
you will not take warmth
from cold churches or soup kitchens,
instead, for long periods, you will
exasperate would-be poets with illusions,
in the reference room of the Galway County Library.

I started with Heaney,
you started to cough.
You coughed all the way to Ormsby,
I was on the verge of Mahon.

Daunted, I left you the Ulster Poets
to consume or cough at.

I moved to the medical section.

Evangeline

Evangeline,
God help her,
reacts to macho men,
who in the end
expect her to survive
on the draught
of far-flung embraces,

not interested in
her food-mixer
philosophies,
her many ways
with crux pastry.

Only wanting
what she can never
give freely.

Look Evan, through
your stainless net curtains,
another far-flung embrace –
take it,

opium for the dead
self that leads
to seven second security.

She had notions,
some dreary Tuesdays,
about swish red
sports cars
and a villa
off the something
coast of France.

She saw herself
in a plunging neckline,
offering her condolences
to Anthony Quinn
Lee Marvin types.

Much later
that same lifetime,
when the kids are asleep,
she crawls out
of her apron pocket
and meets herself
for the first time that day
in the eyes of Martha Glynn,
ten *Silk Cut*
and a small white sliced.

'Will we see you
on the bingo bus
a Friday, Martha G?'

'I wouldn't miss it
for the world.'
And out of her mouth
came all the eights,
and she brought laughter
to all in Folan's shop
for the second
time this month.

Mrs McEttigan

No coincidence was this,
it was arranged by God,
you would say.

Me, posting a letter.
You, you were just there.

You, from somewhere in Ulster,
I loved your accent.
Me, from somewhere in space,
you loved my mother.

You always said the same thing
'Your mother is in Heaven,
she was a saint, God be good to her.'

You lifted your eyes.

You, with the posh brooch,
two stones missing, your Mass hat.

I was just there.

Don't ever die, Mrs McEttigan,
I need to see you outside the Post Office
sending glances to a saint.

Tommy's Wife

She wasn't always this bitter,
I knew her when she sang in pubs.

She was younger then and free,
a happy life she spent.

Working in Woolworths,
she kept herself well. Blue eye shadow.

She married for the sake of the kid.
A lot of envelopes she received. The day.

It started out well for her
the family stood by her then.

Tommy looks strong, many friends,
likes Guinness, sex and unemployment.

She lost blue eye-shadow first year,
Sara now five months, teething hard.

She didn't sing in pubs any more,
she wasn't as friendly as before.

The other three children didn't delay,
she remembered wearing blue eye-shadow.

The coal man hated calling now,
he didn't understand her anger.

Tommy looks strong, many friends,
likes Guinness, sex and unemployment.

Unnecessary Work

(for Bernie)

Sunday evening
we walked
unwanted calories
into the prom
for leisure.

Our duty now
homeward-bound
to visit the mother's grave.

On an unkempt plot nearby
a community of pink carnations
overpowers me.

'You won't have luck for it,'
my sister said.

Later on they stood
in a black Chinese vase
accompanied by
one blooming spike
of white gladiolus
the cat had broken off.

Their agreeable essence
adds life to this room.
I mime a hurried
prayer for the repose
of the soul of
Mary Elizabeth Cooke.

Work On

Nostalgia takes me back –
the shirt factory toilet.

Where country girls met
and sucked cigarette ends on Monday mornings.

Sunday night was discussed, the Ranch House,
his acreage, physique and the make of his car.

Precisely they swayed to and fro,
tannoy blasted sweet lyrics, their hero.

Two jived to the beat, two killed the smoke
and seven sank further into hand-basins.

Boisterous laughter echoed and betrayed lost time.
'Back to work girls,' supervisor sang.

A thousand buttonholes today.
A thousand Ranch House fantasies the weekend.

Work On.

The Apprentices

Daily they perch
during factory lunchtimes
on their man-made Olympus.

Who will attempt to pass
through their veil of lust unscathed
by Henry Leech-along's recital
of his nine favourite adjectives?

Hardly the unprotected townie
shielded only by the active ingredients
of a lifetime's venial sins.

Maybe some young one from the Tech,
the brazen Bridget variety –
mother in a home,
father in a bottle.

Hey you! Wearers of brown acrylic pullovers,
a yellow stripe across your chest-bone
means your mother is still alive,
think not of other people's undertones,
of milk-white flesh, of touching thighs.

AnCo never trained you for this.

Stay awhile, Pavlovian pets, fill your sights
with more ambitious things,
like when your apprenticeship ends
and you are released on the world
a qualified this or that.

Right now you are an apprentice's echo,
know your station.

Power Cut

Black-out excitement, enchanting,
chasing shadows up and down.

Delirious children play scary
monsters, the walls laugh back.

Father bear sleeps it off,
dreams of good westerns.

Mother bear thinks it cultural,
collects young, reads by candle shade.

Siblings content, maternal wing snug,
drifting softly, land of mild and honey.

Father bear slept enough, weary of culture,
'Try the lights upstairs,' he shouts.

Mother bear switches on. Another culture shock,
westerns, yoghurt and the late news.

Poetry Doesn't Pay

People keep telling me:
Your poems, you know,
you've really got something there,
I mean really.

When the rent man calls, I go
down on my knees, and through
the conscience box I tell him,

'This is somebody speaking,
short distance, did you know
I have something here with my poems?
People keep telling me.'

'All I want is fourteen pounds
and ten pence, hold the poesy.'

'But don't you realise
I've got something here.'

If you don't come across
with fourteen pounds and ten pence soon
you'll have something at the side of the road,
made colourful by a little snow.'

'But.'

'But nothing,
you can't pay me in poems or prayers
or with your husband's jokes,
or with photographs of your children
in lucky lemon sweaters
hand-made by your dead grand aunt
who had amnesia and the croup.

'I'm from the Corporation,
what do we know or care about poesy,
much less grand amnostic dead aunts.'

'But people keep telling me.'

'They lie.'

'If you don't have fourteen pounds
and ten pence, you have nothing
but the light of the penurious moon.'

Goddess on the Mervue Bus

Aphrodite
of the homely bungalow,
cross curtains,
off-white Anglia at the side.

Your father
(who is no Zeus)
turns old scrap
into rolled gold
nightly from memory,

looks down on you
from his scap mountain,
hurling forks of caution
about the tin-can man

who fumbles in the aisle
of the Mervue bus,
longing for the chance
of a throwaway smile,
a discarded bus ticket.

O Goddess on the Mervue bus,
no scrap dealer fashioned
you from memory or want,
you were spun from golden
dust, a dash of dream.

Enslaver of mortals,
you choose me.

Once when you yawned
I saw myself
sitting cross-legged
on a lonely molar
waiting for the crunch.

The German for Stomach
(for Eva)

I was waiting for the twenty-past
in the rain, trying to think
of the German for stomach.

While I was racking,
I took time out for
a stew fantasy.
When a blue Merc pulled
out in front of a brown Mini,
I had stew fantasy interruptus.

The man in the brown Mini
was blue and furious
but he didn't let on.
Poor Rex later that day.

The blue Merc made me think
of blue skies and blue seas,
then it came to me.
Bauch, that's it, der Bauch.
I said to myself all the way home,
except when I passed the graveyard,
time for another stew fantasy.

I got off near Kane's butchers.
Inside they were discussing
the gimp and colour of Sean Sweeney's
duodenum when the doctor opened him.
They called it the Northern Province.

It was on the tip of my tongue
and out it tumbled.
'Bauch is the German for stomach.'

His wife said,
'Are you sure you don't want
a carrier bag for that, loveen?'

I could see that
the butcher was overwhelmed,
he wanted to shout
Lapis Lazuli, Lapis Lazuli,
but instead he said,

'You wouldn't put a dog out in it.'

Almost Communication

My father just passed me
in his Fiat 127
I was cycling my bicycle 'Hideous'.

They stopped at O'Meara's
for the *Connacht Tribune*.
As I passed I shouted
'road hog' in the window.

The occupants laughed.

Before this he owned
a Renault 12,
we called it
the 'Ballyhaunis cow killer'.

Later we met outside the sister's,
'Wouldn't you think
he'd buy you a decent bike, the miser.'

'If he had your money,' I said
and we laughed.

The neighbours with their ears
to the rose bushes
think that we're great friends.

I haven't seen his eyes for years.

Middle-aged Irish Mothers

Germinating sopranos in conservative head squares
are the middle-aged Irish mothers in heavy plaid
coats, who loiter after Mass in churches,

    Lord make me an instrument of your peace;
    Where there is hatred, let me sow love;

to light candles for the Joes and Tommies of the drinking world,
the no-hopers, that they might pack it in,
if it's the will of God,

    Where there is injury, pardon;
    Where there is discord, union;

to pray for Susan's safe delivery, Bartley's gambling,
Mrs Murray's veins, that they would not bother her
so much, not forgetting Uncle Matt's shingles.

    Where there is doubt, faith;
    Where there is despair, hope;

Soon, not out of boredom, they will move diagonally
through their cruciform sanctuary to do the Stations
in echoing semi-song whispers,

    We adore thee O Christ we bless thee,
    because by thy cross thou hast redeemed the world;

sincere pleas to dear Jesus, that the eldest might
get off with a light sentence, pledges of no more smoking,
and guarantees of attendance at the nine Fridays,

    Where there is darkness, light;
    Where there is sadness, joy;

finally, for the Pope's intentions, Mr Glynn's brother-in-law,
the sweeps ticket that it might come up, but only if it's the will of
    God,

O Sacred Heart of Jesus, I place
all my trust and confidence in thee.

I like these middle-aged Irish mothers, in heavy plaid coats,
one of them birthed me on the eve of a saint's feast day,
with a little help from Jesus and his Sacred Heart.

Ode to Rahoon Flats

O Rahoon, who made you
to break the hearts
of young girls with
pregnant dreams

of an end terrace,
crisp white clothes
lines and hire purchase
personalities?

You don't care if her
children crawl into her
curved spine,
distort her thinking.

You put Valium on a
velvet cushion
in the form of a
juicy red apple.

Rahoon, why are you
so cruel to young
husbands, hooked on
your butter voucher

bribes? If you crumbled
would it take three days
or would the ground swallow
you up, payment for your sins?

The Long Ward

I have never seen
an old woman
eating an orange.

The long ward
for the old
and sometimes
the odd appendix.

The long ward
for craic,
for prayer,
a joke, a song
and sometimes pain.

In the long ward
Silvermints are
shared and returned
with photographs of
'My second eldest'
or 'This one is in Canada'.

Some come to visit,
to care, to love,
few to count acres
in old women's eyes.

In the long ward
it pleases when
the priest passes
your bed.

In the dead of night
a cry for somebody's son.
No welcome for the grey
box that comes to call.

Thin legs you see,
smiling mothers
in new Dunnes dressing-gowns,
new slippers,
boxes of tissues
they would never use at home.

Always one to joke
about the black doctor,
always one to complain
about the cold tea, no ham.

An eye on the clock,
a hand on the rosary beads,
pain well out of sight.

The loved grandchildren
embrace good-looking oranges
and ancient smiles.

God-of-the-Hatch Man

(for Community Welfare Officers everywhere)

Smoking and yes mamming,
snoozing in the fright
of his altered expression,
caused always by the afternoon.

Tepid water sipper, coffee glutton,
pencil pointer, negative nouner,
God-of-the-hatch man, hole in the wall.

We call religiously every Thursday,
like visiting the holy well,
only this well purports to give you things
instead of taking them away.

Things like scarlatina, schizophrenia,
migraine, hisgraine but never your grain,
lockjaw and wind, silicosis,
water on the knee, hunger in the walletness.

We queue for an hour or three,
we love to do this,
our idea of pleasure,
Then whatever-past what-past he likes,
he appears.

Tepid water sipper, coffee glutton,
pencil pointer, negative nouner,
God-of-the-hatch man, hole in the wall.

He gives us money and abuse,
the money has a price,
the abuse is free.

'Are you sure your husband isn't working?'
'Are you sure grumbling granny is quite dead?'
'Are you sure you're not claiming for de Valera?'
'Are you sure you count six heads in every bed?'

Hummer of Andy Williams' tunes,
most talked about man in the waiting-room,
tapper of the pencil on the big brown desk.

God-of-the-hatch man, hole in the wall.
God-of-the-hatch man, hole in the wall.

Mona

Mona doesn't die here
any more, she lives
in a house at the back
of her mind.

Some place small,
cosy and warm,
fully detached,
a single storey,
with no gable ending,
a high wall
but no door.

Away from
tenants' associations,
rent man's,
poor man's,
light bills,
heavy bills,
free newspapers,
and six-year-old perpetrators on skates.

When she was here
she was afraid
of salutations,
candied appreciations,
of tendon squeezing
politicians
who didn't care.

In supermarkets
she was tricked by
pennies off here,
free holidays over there,
buy three and get
anxiety for nothing.

She was a coupon saver,
she saved them
but they never saved her.

Mona doesn't die there
any more, she lives
in a shed at the back
of her house.

Some place small,
cosy and warm,
a high wall
but no door.

Sunny Side Plucked

We met outside
the seconds chicken
van at the market.

He was very American,
I was very married.

We chatted about
the home-made marmalade
I bought two miles
from home.

He said the eggs were big,
I said he'd been eating
his carrots.

'Do you always buy
seconds chickens?'

'Only when I come late.'

The witch in me
wanted to scramble
his eggs.

The devil in him
wanted to pluck
my chicken.

We parted
with an agreement
written by the eyes.

FROM **WITCH
IN THE BUSHES**

(1988)

It's All Because We're Working-Class
(for Michael A.)

Through them
you could see
no rhyme reason
or gable end;
that coal bag washer
and grass eater
from the Shantalla clinic
prescribed them.

Burn your patch
he said
and be a man;
slip these on
and see into
the souls of men;
and our Ambrose
walked into
the gable end
and his life
was in splinters
thereafter.

All he really needed
was to rest his lazy eye
for a few months
and the wrong eye
would right itself.

It's like having your leg
tied behind your back
for six years
then suddenly have it released
and be told,
go now and breakdance
on a tight-rope.

It's all because we're working-class;
if we lived up in Taylor's Hill
with the coal bag washers
and grass eaters,
do you think for one minute
they would put
them big thick spy-glasses on your child?

Not a tall
not a fuckin' tall;
they'd give ya them film star glasses
with the glitter on them,
just as sure
as all their metallic purple wheelbarrows
have matching cocker spaniels
they would;

fuckin' coal bag washers
and grass eaters
the whole fuckin' lot of them;
and it's all because we're working-class.

She Is Not Afraid of Burglars

(for Leland B.)

It's lunchtime
and he's training the dog again.
He says to the dog in a cross voice,
'Stay there.'
The dog obeys him.

When he goes home
he forgets to leave the cross voice
in the green where he trains his dog
and spits out unwoven troubles
that won't fit in his head.

He says to his wife,
'Stay there.'
His wife obeys him.
She sees how good he is with the dog
and how the dog obeys his cross voice.

She boasts to the locals,
'I would never be afraid of burglars
with my husband in the house.'

The locals, busting for news, ask her,
'Why would you never be afraid of burglars
with your husband in the house?'

She calls a meeting at Eyre Square
for half three that Saturday.
Standing on a chair, wiping her hands
on her apron, she explains.

'One day,' she says, in a cross voice,
'The dog disobeyed my husband
and my husband beat him across the head
with a whip made from horse hair.

That is why I am not afraid of burglars
with my husband in the house.'

It Wasn't the Father's Fault

His father
him hit
with a baseball bat
and he was
never right since.

Some say
he was never right
anyway.

Standing
behind the kitchen table
one Sunday before Mass
his mother said,

'If Birdie Geary
hadn't brought
that cursed baseball bat
over from America,

none of this would have happened.'

The Did-You-Come-Yets of the Western World

When he says to you:
You look so beautiful
you smell so nice –
how I've missed you –
and did you come yet?

It means nothing,
and he is smaller
than a mouse's fart.

Don't listen to him...
Go to Annaghdown Pier
with your father's rod.
Don't necessarily hold out
for the biggest one;
oftentimes the biggest ones
are the smallest in the end.

Bring them all home,
but not together.
One by one is the trick;
avoid red herrings and scandal.

Maybe you could take two
on the shortest day of the year.
Time is the cheater here
not you, so don't worry.

Many will bite the usual bait;
they will talk their slippery way
through fine clothes and expensive perfume,
fishing up your independence.

These are
the did-you-come-yets of the western world,
the feather and fin rufflers.
Pity for them they have no wisdom.

Others will bite at any bait.
Maggot, suspender, or dead worm.
Throw them to the sharks.

In time one will crawl
out from under thigh-land.
Although drowning he will say,

'Woman I am terrified, why is this house
shaking?'

And you'll know he's the one.

Be Someone

(for Carmel)

For Christ's sake,
learn to type
and have something
to fall back on.

Be someone,
make something of yourself,
look at Gertrudo Ganley.

Always draw the curtains
when the lights are on.

Have nothing to do
with the Shantalla gang,
get yourself a right man
with a Humber Sceptre.

For Christ's sake
wash your neck
before going into God's house.

Learn to speak properly,
always pronounce your ings.
Never smoke on the street,
don't be caught dead
in them shameful tight slacks,

spare the butter,
economise,

and for Christ's sake
at all times,
watch your language.

Old Soldier

He stood
at the top
of Shop Street
cursing de Valera
and he muttered
something about
the Blueshirts
and when he saw
Mrs Flanagan, he said,
'You could have
got worse than me,
but you wanted
a fisherman didn't ya?
I wasn't always
like this,' he said,
and his veins broke
and he died alone
but not lonely,
for many's the revolution
he fought in his scullery
with his newspaper
and his fine words.

Witch in the Bushes

(for Padraic Fiacc)

I know a man
who tried
to eat a rock
a big rock
grey and hard,
unfriendly too.

Days later
he is still grinding,
the rock
is not getting
any smaller.

Because of this
rock in the jaw,
this impediment,
the man has become
even more angry.

No one
could look at him,
but a few
hard cases did.
They were mostly dockers;
they reckoned,

'We have seen
the savage seas
rise over our dreams,
we can look
at a bull-head
eating a rock'.

The years passed
slowly and painfully,
until one day
the rock was no more,
neither was much of the man.

He didn't
grind the rock down,
the rock
hammered a job
on him and his ego.

Then, one day
an old woman
came out of the bushes
wearing a black patch
and a questionnaire,
in her wand hand
she held a posh red pencil,
well pared.

She questioned him
between wheezes
(she had emphysema
from smoking damp tobacco
and inhaling fumes
from her open fire
in the woods)
if all that anger
for all those years
was worth it.

Old Rockie Jaw
couldn't answer
he had forgotten
the reason
and the cause.

He concluded
'Anger is OK
if you spill it,
but chewing
is assuredly
murder on the teeth.'

He had learned
his lesson
he would
pull himself together
smarten up like,
turn the other cheek,
he would go easy
on the oils that aged him.

Every now and then
he weakened,
he let the voice
from the rock take over,
an army voice
with a militant tone,

'A man is a man
and a real man
must spit feathers
when the occasion arises.'

Like all good voices
this one
had an uncle,
it was the voice
of the uncle
that bothered him,
it always
had the same warning,

'About
the witch in the bushes,'
it said,
'Watch her,
she never sleeps.'

Anything Is Better than Emptying Bins
(for Jessie)

I work at the Post Office.
I hate my job,
but my father said
there was no way
I could empty bins
and stay under his roof.

So naturally,
I took a ten week
extra-mural course
on effective stamp-licking;
entitled
'More lip and less tongue.'

I was mostly unpleasant,
but always under forty
for young girls
who bought stamps with hearts
for Valentine's Day.

One day a woman asked me
could she borrow a paper-clip,
she said something about
sending a few poems away
and how a paper-clip
would make everything so much neater.

But I've met the make-my-poems-neater-type before;
give in to her once,
and she'll be back in a week asking,
'Have you got any stamps left over?'

Well I told her where to get off.
'Mrs Neater-poems,' I said,
'this is a Post Office
not a friggin' card shop,
and if you want paper-clips
you'll get a whole box full
across the street for twenty pence.'

Later when I told my father,
he replied,
'Son, it's not how I'd have handled it,
but anything is better than emptying bins.'

Second Thoughts

It is better
not to tell
your best friend
that you have
a lover.

Because
in fourteen days
you might say
to yourself,

I should not
have told her.
Then you will go
to her house

even though
your shoes
are hurting you,
you will say to her,

my best friend,
remember
what I was telling you
fourteen days ago
at half past five,

well it's not true
I made it up
just for fun,
so forget
I ever mentioned it.

But when
you get to her house
you find
she is not in,
in fact
you find her out.

So you go
to her place of work,
she works
at the sausage factory.

People
in a small group
at the main gate say,

'She is not here
and you
can't find her in
when she is out,
you must
find her out.'

They tell you this
in a sing song way,
she has gone
to the doctor's

they say it
four times
for no reason.

You wonder
if she
has told them,
you wonder
if they
are looking at you funny
and when you pass
are they saying
to themselves,
in their
older sisters' dresses,

'There she goes
that slut,
she should be
in the sausage factory,
she should be
a sausage.'

By the time
you reach the doctor's
she has left,
you are sweating
on the road
through your clothes
into your
tight-fitting shoes.

You wonder
if keeping your secret
has made her sick
and that is why
she is at the doctor's.

You take the bus
to her house
you are there
before she opens
the front gate,

you are disappointed
when her mother tells you
through their squint window
that she has gone back to work

to make up
the time
she lost
whilst going
to the doctor's
for a prescription
for her father's
catarrh.

You decide
there and then
to take out an ad
in the local paper,

telling her
to forget all you said
that Saturday
fourteen days ago
at half past five.

She is
more than pleased;
to your face
she tells you
the next time
you meet,

she adds to this
without blinking
that you won't mind
if she goes out
with the man

you never
had the affair with
as he had been
asking her
for seven months.

And you
look round the town
you have dragged
your dirty linen through

from her house
to the sausage
to the doctor's
to the mother's

And you look up
and down the long
narrow streets
of the town you
were born in

and you wonder.

He Fought Pigeons' Arses, Didn't He?

And she pissed
in his toilet
and ate his sausages
and he said
there was nothing
but lust between them.

And on his day off
he got an aerosol
and he wanted to spray
the arses of dead pigeons black.

And he said to her
'If it's war you want
I'll give you war.
We'll have our own war,
spraying the arses of dead pigeons black
and we'll fight seven days out of six.

And the seventh day of the six
we'll discuss the situation,
and I'll bet you
twenty black pigeons' arses
there'll still be nothing
but lust between us.'

I Went to School with You

My children call her
Dolly Partners
and I don't check them.

Sometimes
when I'm well fed
and satisfied in every other way
and they say it,
we all laugh.

One night when I was coming home
from Mick Taylor's, half pie-eyed,
she called me.

She had no pies in her eyes
and no flies either
she spoke with her finger
her index finger,
but she never danced with the afternoon
the sunny afternoon.

1t's your duty as a mother
to control your children,'
said the finger, the index finger.
'When you are out'
('which is often,' she muttered under her manacles)
'I can hear nothing
but Madonna blaring and your youngest swearing.'

'And furthermore,' said another voice,
in an Italian accent (but we couldn't hear it)

'You miserable hag,
you never speak with your finger
your index finger,
and shame on you
you often dance with the afternoon
the sunny afternoon.
How dare you, how absolutely dare you.'

After that the finger came back on duty,
it was the index finger
and it was night duty
and it was her duty.

And the killing part of it all is, it said,

I went to school with you.

End of a Free Ride

For years
my cousin never charged me
on the bus.

One day he said to my sister,
'Your wan would need to watch herself
stickin' up for the knackers.'

After that he went home
and had pig's cheek and cabbage,
lemon swiss roll and tea.

He called out to his wife Annie
(who was in the scullery steeping
the shank for Thursday)

'Annie love get us the milk,
was I tellin' ya,
I'll have to start chargin' my cousin
full fare from here on in.'

'Why's that?' said Annie love
returning with the milk.

'Cos she's an adult now, that's why.'

The Tell Tattler

Have you anything
to tell us today
tell tattler?

Did you help any
old woman across
a crowded street?

Did you spread
your Sunday coat in muck
for any dainty foot?

In a pub
spacious enough
for dreamers with hope,
not near enough
to Annaghmakerrig,
you can meet the tell tattler
with a gold pelican pinned to his lapel.

Without coaxing
or pain he will tell you
about the blood he has given over the years.

He was a school teacher once.
He put streams of children into his wife,
but they fell out again uneducated and sour.

In time they shouted
from sinking Monaghan hills,
'Where is our blood-giving father now,
our chest pounder and coat spreader?
We no longer see his polished pelican
shining in the distance.

Your falling out children need to check;
that you have tells to tattle,
that you have an endless supply
of unwilling old women to drag across busy streets,
that you have cloth enough for the dainty foot,
that you have good hearing for when the bell tolls,
that you are not, our father, running out of blood.'

Woman's Inhumanity to Woman

(Galway Labour Exchange)

And in this cage, ladies and gentlemen,
we have the powers that be.

Powder power,
lipstick power,
pencil power,
paper power,
cigarette in the left-hand power,
raised right of centre half-plucked eyebrow,
Cyclops power,
big tits power,
piercing eyes power,
filed witches' nails power,
I own this building power,
I own you power,
fear of the priest power,
fear of the Black 'n' Tans power.

Your father drank too much power,
your sister had a baby when she was fifteen power,
where were you last night power,
upstairs in your house is dirty power,
the state of your hotpress power,
the state of your soul power,
keep door closed power,
keep eyes closed power,
no smoking power,
money for the black babies power,
queue only here power,
sign only there power,
breathe only when I tell you power.

No pissing on the staff power,
jingle of keys power,
your brother signs and works power,
ye have a retarded child power,
you sign and work power,
look over your shoulder power,
look over your brother's shoulder power,
I know your mother's maiden name power,
look at the ground power,
I know your father's maiden name power,
spy in the sky power,
spy in the toilet power,
fart in front of a bishop power.

Apologise for your mother's colour hair power,
apologise for your father's maiden name power,
apologise for being born power.

The Blanket Man

He calls
in his
new Volvo
collecting
the pound a week.

Him and his Volvo.

Sometimes
if she can't pay
he says,
'C'mon, c'mon missus,
if it was my stuff
I'd let you have it
for nothing.'

Leaning against
the door jamb
she doesn't
believe him.

Her and her cigarette.

No Balls at All

The cats in Castle Park
are shameless,
they talk dirty all night long;
but not our Fluffy.

Our cat had been de-railed,
(that's Czechoslovakian for neutered)
but he doesn't know it.

He gets flashbacks
from his desire-filled past;
often along our back wall
he tiptoes tamely chasing pussy;

when he gets to the point of no return
he gets a blackout,
he well knows with his acute cat sense
that the next bit is the best bit,
but he just can't remember
what he is supposed to do.

He was an alley-cat-and-a-half once,
but felines complained,
not softly but oftenly
about his overzealous scratchy nature;
so we took him to the vet
where his desire was taken;
snapped at, whipped off, wiped out
by a man in a white coat.

It was sad really,
de-railed in body but not fully in mind;
would he ever get over it,
our cat with some desire and no equipment?

Days now
he just sits
inside our white lace curtain
envying his promiscuous alley-cat friends.

Other times,
he plays with a ball of blue wool
or a grey rubber mouse
throwing him in the air
letting on to be tough.

Still, he would have his memories,
they would come and visit him
teasing him back
to the tumbling times of testiclehood;

but sadly for the de-railed alley-cat
there is no second coming;
we came to accept it, and so did our Fluffy.

Peter Picasso

Feeding on
potatoes and onions
and heating himself
from stolen coal
and migraine memories
of a day flush with
carrot-weight friends
and apple song,
this Protestant painter lives.

'Take out someone's appendix
make someone's teeth sing
design a hideous church,
but for the love and honour
of all that is holy
stay away from the evil easel,
that's only for the death-coloured
do-fuck-all dandified doters
who'd cut off your ear
as quick as they'd look at you.'

Peter Picasso
who could well hear
but didn't listen
let his brush take him
to this chicken shite wall world
next to Moo-hat post office,
where the crows ate the priest.*
His fall is broken
and so is his heart
when an art student in tight jeans
meanders through his chicken shite world.

He conjures her up
before and after feeds
and provided it's not too wet
and she swears not to step on his wolfhound,
she can glide with him
in and out of the heads of cows
and more things less political.

66

And on cold winter nights
she can dance
on his stolen coal fire,
while he laughs at the walls
and checks that both ears are still there.

* A Christy Higgins line.

Some People
(for Eoin)

Some people know what it's like,

to be called a cunt in front of their children
to be short for the rent
to be short for the light
to be short for school books
to wait in Community Welfare waiting-rooms full of smoke
to wait two years to have a tooth looked at
to wait another two years to have a tooth out (the same tooth)
to be half strangled by your varicose veins, but you're
198th on the list
to talk into a banana on a jobsearch scheme
to talk into a banana in a jobsearch dream
to be out of work
to be out of money
to be out of fashion
to be out of friends
to be in for the Vincent de Paul man
to be in space for the milk man
(sorry, mammy isn't in today she's gone to Mars for the weekend)
to be in Puerto Rico this week for the blanket man
to be in Puerto Rico next week for the blanket man
to be dead for the coal man
(sorry, mammy passed away in her sleep, overdose of coal
in the teapot)
to be in hospital unconscious for the rent man
(St Judes ward 4th floor)
to be second-hand
to be second-class
to be no class
to be looked down on
to be walked on
to be pissed on
to be shat on

and other people don't.

They Believe in Clint Eastwood

In Cork prison
on Ash Wednesday
the warders have
black crosses painted
where the Cyclops
had his eye.

They believe in
the Trinity,

They believe in
reincarnation,

They believe in
dust and ashes,

They believe in
Jesus with long hair,

They believe in
Clint Eastwood,

They believe in
key consortium;

They believe in
the letter of the law.

God Dodgers Anonymous

The Jehovah Witness
asked her
if she had a God.

No beating
around the burning bush
for this lassie.
Straight from the hip,
eyeball to eyeball job.

Have you a God?

It depends
on how you look at it,
I haven't a pot to spew libations in
yet the Gods are hopping up
all over the joint,

and funny thing
it's never
with chalice and host,
it's always
with book and pen;
sometimes a sugary grin.

'I'm God
give us four pounds
or I'll kick
your shite in.'

The Witness
witnessing a new line
in idolatry,
was flummoxed.

She told the one
who was beyond saving
to have a nice day
(she said it twice for effect).

I will, she assured,
I'll have a bastarding ball
dodging the Gods
round the grand piano
that isn't really there at all,

spitting fire
awaiting the second coming,
and when I'm not fasting for fun
I can always spend an hour or two

chewing the Moroccan sturdite binding
off the Book of Daniel
and before you can say
'Watch out for the Watchtower,'

I'll see the three horsemen of the Apocalypse
(the fourth is having a hip operation)
strutting in here, proffering
gold, frankincense and more.

Every Second Sunday

'Can't talk now
I'm rushing up
to pay the raffle,

"The Cashel Circle"

I owe two weeks.

If I won
that hundred
no bill-boy
would get a shaggin' penny
that's for sure.

I'd buy myself
two pairs of shoes,
shop shoes,
I'd wear them

every second Sunday.'

Him and His Terrier

The demons
made his fists dance,
no lamp-post was safe.

Before this
he was fussy about
who he said hello to.
No Eastsider would ever get
his greeting.

All his stories had
Atlantic Ocean connections;
a sailor in his heart
but he never left town.

They sought him out
for his good conversation,
it was water water everywhere.

He got worse
the stories got better
more sea, less land.
He went further away
still he never left town.

They say his brain
got sizzled with the booze.
Methylated Spirits in the end,
it stole his conversation
no more fights with lampposts.

Not fussy about Eastsiders now,
his words are few, but he repeats them.
Hello to everyone from the corner,
him and his terrier.

Reading

To a group of prisoners
in a locked room
with a cage at the back.
It housed a warder
who lay across two chairs.

When he got restless
or peckish
he pranced up and down
in his new shoes
(they were always new
because they rarely touched ground).

'Slouched warder hears poetry
in horizontal position.'

A volunteer
made me tea,
chocolate biscuits
offered.

I read,
they listened
the one in the cage yawned
an uninterested-in-poetry yawn
(I know an uninterested-in-poetry yawn
a mile off; I interpret them).

I read some more,
a volley of questions,
some comments,
explosive laughter escaped
time and time again.

Their hunger for knowledge
stalked between lines of poems,
behind falling vowels,
in and out of hooks of question-marks
under jaded asterisks;

they wanted to know
they wanted to know.

Seconds galloped all over us
minutes ricocheted
two hours shot by,
we were all casualties.

With the jingle of keys
I was free to go
handshakes, smiles
much left unsaid,

the distance between us
several poems shorter.

I feared the man in the cage.

Philomena's Revenge

As a teenager
she was like any other,
boys, the craic,
smoking down the backs.

Later there was talk
she broke things,
furniture and glass,
her mother's heart.

'Mad at the world,'
the old women nod
round each other's faces.

But it was more
than that
and for less
she was punished.

That weekend
she didn't leave a cup alone
every chair hit the wall,
Philomena's revenge.

Soon after
she was shifted
and given the shocks.

Round each other's faces
the old women nod,
'Treatment, treatment
they've given her the treatment.'

These days
she gets on with the furniture,
wears someone else's walk,
sees visions in glass.

She's good too
for getting the messages;
small things, bread and milk
sometimes the paper,

and closing the gate
after her father drives out,
she waits for his signal
he always shouts twice,

'Get the gate Philo,
get the gate, girl.'

People Who Wear Cardigans Are Subversive

People who wear cardigans
are the type of people
who say,

'Would you get us
the Gold Flake
out of the cardi in the hall stand
before the race starts
like a good girl.'

People who wear cardigans are subversive.

I know a man who swore
'All popes are good.'
He was a C wearer.

They are more likely
to call their children strange names.
I knew one with a sly neck
who had a habit of saying
out of the corner of his mouth,
'J.C.B. Kellogg and Dry Bread
your tea is ready.'
He was a seven day a week C wearer.

They keep their money
and bits of granny
in biscuit tins
under the stairs.
They pray for rain
and the postponement of Christmas,
plus the evacuation of all children
to the plural of Pluto.

People who wear cardigans are subversive.

They harbour resentments against
slickless phones.

I knew a heavy breather once,
when leaving the scene
he said into the smutty night air,

'Here I am,
full of ooohs and aaahs
and the phone is jammed.'
He was a two a day C wearer.

Other C wearers
wear socks with sandals,
it goes with the territory,
'Keep the lungs
and the soles of the feet hot
and the rest will take care of itself,'
a C wearer's motto.

They get up before themselves,
get down before no one,
never shoot themselves in the foot,
but in caution
keep all loose legs under the table.

People who wear cardigans are subversive.

They wear them to hide things,
like biscuit tins,
granny bits,
rain storms,
lost Christmases,
protruding calendars,
and deep resentments.

People who wear cardigans are subversive.

Born agains and born liars
the lot of them.
One swears his grandfather could do a wheelie
while a suppressed piano
wavered on his altered ego,
he was a C wearer.

Cravat merchants
with skull rings at the gullet,
devil worshippers,
Claddagh ringers,
duffle coaters, bin lidders.

People who wear cardigans are subversive.

Misogynist

Is the boss in?
Could he give us
a yard of a tow,

the engine's after
collapsin' on me again,
she is, the bitch.

The Deserter

He couldn't wait
just up and died
on me.

Two hours,
two hours
I spent ironing
them shirts
and he didn't even
give me the pleasure
of dirtying them,

that's the type
of person he was,
would rather die
than please you.

But in his favour
I will say this for him,
he made a lovely corpse.
Looked better dead
than he did in our front room
before the telly,

right cock-of-the-walk
in that coffin,
head slightly tilted back
like he was going to say
'My dear people.'

He couldn't wait,
never,
like the time
before the All-Ireland
we were going to Mass,

he had to have a pint
or he'd have the gawks, he said.

That's the type he was,
talk dirty in front of any woman.

No stopping him
when he got that ulcer out,
but where did it get him,

wax-faced above
in the morgue
that's where.

He's not giving
out to me now
for using Jeyes Fluid
on the kitchen floor,

or stuffing the cushions
with his jaded socks...
and what jaded them?
Pub crawling jaded them,
that's what.

He's tight-lipped now
about my toe separators,
before this
he would threaten them
on the hot ash.

The next time
I spend two hours
ironing shirts for him
he'll wear them.

Questionnaire After Leaving Aillwee Cave

Does your dog bite?
(land owner, working-class,
jumped-up third generation
guttersnipe or other)

How many full stops in *The Gulag Archipelago*?

Do you wear coloured condoms?
(green, purple, gold, black or other)

Do you think Boris Yeltsin and Teresa of the Little
Flower are the same person?

Do you wear two at a time?

Do you see the humour in unemployment?

Do you believe Elvis is still alive?

Should we have free coal?

Did you have dark thoughts in the cave?

What colour should it be?

Spell Acetylsalicylic acid.

Does your wife beat you?
(yes, no, not sure)

Did you ever have impure thoughts about cheese?

Do you ride buses?

About Bree, I see mmmmmmm.
Do you believe in the power of the reflexologist?

Do all Roses of Tralee who don't make it
join the I.R.A.?

Does it hurt...no, no this is the bus question, wake up.

Do you give good phone?

Does your car own you?

Does your Credit Union own you?

Did you want to reach out
and touch someone in the cave?

Was it God?

Good.

Light of the Moon

Question:
Can you tell me
the way to the maternity?

Answer:
Walk on a beach
in the West of Ireland
at four in the morning
in the middle of summer
with a man who's six foot two
and you'll get there
sooner or later.

Question:
Is his height the problem?

Answer:
No, the problem rises
when you stop
to look at the moon.

Question:
So is the moon
the problem?

Answer:
No, not the moon itself
but the glare from the moon
which makes you say
in seagull Russian,
'Fuse me bix foot skew
in your stocking wheat
bould you kind werribly
if I jay on the bat of my flack
for the bext three-quarters of a bour
the boon is milling me.'

Question:
And that's the answer?

Answer:
No, that's the question.
When he lies on top of you
for the next three-quarters of an hour
shielding you from the light of the moon
the answer comes to you.

Question:
Like a flash?

Answer.
No, like the thundering tide.

Cloud Talker

Two men
are putting a roof
on the neighbour's shed.

They are both tall
very tall,
they look alike
very alike,
they would pass for brothers,
they would pass.

One hardly acknowledges her
(in fact for no bad reason
they don't anything each other).

The other one makes cloud talk

She spies on them
from behind the net curtain
where she flushes out
stale and ancient tea-leaf schemes
from two breakfast cups.

This day without charity,
when she is pegging down
their aggressive sheets,
she says to cloud talker,

'I love a man
as tall as you,
as fair as you,
as blue-eyed as you,
but I can't put my hands
inside his shirt
because he's doing life.'

Just then
no-bad-reason spoke.

'Twin brother,' he said,
'enough of your talk,
you'll bring on the rain.
Throw me that hammer,
let's get on with the nails.

We've already been here
half a lifetime.'

Old Timers

She loves the clockman;
she leans on his shoulder
from her bicycle,
cycling slowly
through a field.

Slightly out of step,
the botched hip job
leaves him
one foot shorter
than the other.

She adores him;
his slight tick-over
his offbeat with time
but never with her heart.

Children have worn a path
for these older lovers,
harmony not always seen,
the eye is good
but the heart is better.

They're heading for the pub now.
She loves the clockman;
she leans on his shoulder
from her bicycle.

On their return,
his short step less noticeable,
harmony more visible
as the falling together starts.

The treasured bicycle
now takes third place;
it trails like an unwanted relative,
uncle somebody.

When they hit home
he'll make the tea,
he'll rub her old feet,
they'll make yes and no sentences
for ages with love,

and if the voice is good
she'll sing out to her clockman
sweet youthful melodies,

making him forget
years, months, days,
minutes, seconds,
ticks, tocks,

until the only down-to-earth sound
is the click of her new teeth
as she whispers, gently,

'Love, oh love,
there's no time like the present.'

His Shoulder Blades and Rome

(for Pat Arthurs)

The prisoner
in one of the cells
on the 4's landing
just under the roof,

can hear the soldiers
jumping up and down
trying to keep warm.

The prisoner
lying back in his bed
is thinking about
his ex-wife Maria,
(once the sunshine of his life),

about the time
he took her on holiday
to the Costa del Sol,
and how they separated
two weeks later.

It's getting colder,
colder than cold.
The soldiers are jumping
non-stop now;
they are freezing.

They are interrupting
his thoughts
about Maria, his ex-wife
(once the sunshine),

about the time
he took her on holidays to the Costa,

where she blew non-stop kisses
between his shoulder blades and Rome
easing the sting of yesterday's sun.

Butter Balls

Mountains of butter voucher recipients
met outside the meat hall
in Mill Street,
to hear misery guts
most miserable minister of miseries
spill the mean beans
about the extension
of the butter voucher scheme.

Oh mean miserable minister
misser of minor misdemeanours
and moving trains,
side tracker,
dirty talker,
spiller of misery,
and mean beans,
extender of butter voucher schemes,
tell us the miserable news.

'Good morning mealies,
it gives me great pleasure
(butter pleasure)
to tell all of you
who met today
outside the meat hall
in Mill Street,
which I nearly missed
owing to a minor misdemeanour,

that I oh miserablist of miseries
have made a meanagerial decision
for your benefit,
I've decided to extend
the butter voucher scheme
for another two years,

P.S. and et cetera.
It gives me minister of most miseries
ever more pleasure
(butter pleasure)
to tell you recipients
of unsocial smellfare,

that the above mentioned
butter voucher or B.V.
as we say at the MTs
has been increased from
54p to 55p per V.'

Dead Dogs and Nations

(for Anne Kennedy)

Other things upset her most
like dead dogs and nations.
Take the Gulf War,
she cried for every side,
it took her over
completely and without mercy.

Night, noon
and every phone call
she was Gulf grieving.

Once at a bus stop
she was overheard saying,
'They're killing my people.'

Her compassion immense;
her heart broke for
dead dogs and nations.

Her family
she cut out
at the greeting card stage,
one happy birthday to you
too many in a long line
of smiling faces
turned her off
she disowned the lot,
right down to the cooing babies

in Matinee coats and white souls.
These baby beauties
who brought out the best in others
did nothing for her.

Once she said out loud,
'Purgatory O Purgatory'
no one knew what she meant.

She didn't believe in innocence
or the power of prayer,
Popes and politicians could sizzle.

She went on caring
for dead dogs and other nations
she over-cared, she over-loved
but not really;

her own backyard
was a dark balloon
full of snakes and razor blades.

It's not that the grass
was always greener,
just it was always
under someone else's foot.

When Kelly's dog died
she broke for good.

I'll Have to Stop Thinking About Sex

(for Tadgh Foley)

People
are beginning
to notice.

Take
the two wans
at the market,
the fish market.

They looked
at each other
then they looked
at me.

Then
one said
to the other,

'Other,
that woman
is holding the French loaf
like it was a fisherman.'

They thought
that I thought
that the French loaf
was a you know what.

But they were wrong
'You know whats'
are often hard to fathom,

fishermen are fishermen
(spongy as earlobes).

The French loaf
was fresh and hot,

the only way
to hold it,
a reasonable way
to cool it.

They were wrong
the two wans,
with their know-your-loaf
philosophies
their all-seeing eyes
their all-fish tales.

Between Them

You only see
good-looking couples
out driving
on a Sunday afternoon.

His hair is blonde,
her eyes are blue.

Between them
they have no broken veins
stretch marks
Guinness guts
fat necks
barrel chests
or swollen ankles.

Between them
they never curse.
His give-away sign
is the way he holds the steering wheel
in the twenty-to-two position.

Her give-away sign
is the sweep of the perfume
she leaves lingering at the traffic lights
where the pedestrians often turn green.

Between them
they never eat fries
red or brown sauce
shanks of anybody
mackerel from the basin.
Putrid, they say, putrid.

Between them
they have no cholesterol in the blood
no coal in the shed,
everything is centrally heated,
it's easier that way

cuts out the middle man
and the mess.
Sometimes
when they are not out
looking good-looking,

between them
you could fit:
two McInerney Homes
three Berlin Walls
Martha Glynn's fantasies
four empty factories (I.D.A.)
seventeen rocket couriers (slightly overweight)
forty-eight good quality reconditioned colour TVs
incalculable curriculum Vs

cat fights
frog fights
bull fights
dog fights
broken hearts
hearts in jars
lost wars
lost teeth
teeth in jars
Pope's intentions
sexist free Bibles
Ceaucescu's wealth
Bush's blushes
tea-leaf prophecy classes
sole-of-the-feet prophecy classes
black-eye prophecy classes
white-of-the-eye prophecy classes
moveable feasts
grow your own cameras
poster poems
dirty water
and murder mysteries.

He Leaves the Ironing Board Open

He likes
crisp white shirts
and Tracey Chapman.
He leaves
the ironing board open
in his mobile home
near the motorway,
so that he is halfway there
if he ever makes the decision
to go out.

He plays
Tracey Chapman
really loud
in his mobile home
near the motorway,
so that he can't hear
the noise of the cars
or the screech of his loneliness
crashing into him
from every side.

Space Invader

(for Louise Hermana)

Hey Missus,
you're the poet,
write a poem
about me,

about the time
I lived
in a toilet
for six months,
no shit girlie.

Nothing to whine
home about
but it was dry
and beggars
can't be choosers.

You're the poet,
the one with
the fancy words,

I'm the one
with the toilet –
they call me
the space invader.

A toilet, a toilet
my kingdom
is a toilet –
give us a poem
or piss off missus.

I'm livin'
on twisted pennies
now,
but not for long,

Christmas
is up
round Moon's corner,
and I'll soon
be livin'
off the hog.

I've an uncle
a docker
full card and all
says there's money
in dirty coal yet,

and the coal boat
has a leak,
know what I mean
girlie missus.

Write a poem
about me
about the time
I lived
in a toilet
for six months.

After all
you're the poet
girlie missus
the one with
the fancy words.

Limits

There were limits
to what he could take
so he took limits,
sometimes he went
over the limits,

other times the limits
went over him,
not in any aggressive way
down the neck way
oil the oesophagus way,

cool and refreshing
on a hot summer's day way;
so he had a problem
he had to watch it.

His mother said it
so did his wife, watch it
the wise ones said, watch it.

But sometimes
when he wasn't looking
limits got him
handcuffed him
forced him into it,
down the neck way
oil the oesophagus way,

when he was
over the limits
nobody wanted him,
he was an unwashed, unwanted,
unwilling, unattractive,
over the limits slob.

He never got wise
he only got older,
the limits got higher
the climb got harder.

He reached nowhere
in jigtime,
anywhere in no time.
He had no limits
no fun, no jokes
no-how, no jumpers

only sitters
who sat around with him
and blamed the grass for growing,
the Government, the I.R.A,
the A.B.C, the I.U.D,
the U.F.O, the I.T.V.
He was a paid up member
of the sitters and blamers gang.

After a while
he had no need
to watch it,
limits now looked
for plump ones
half his measure
who still had fight.

He had fought
all his battles
and lost.
He was a lost limit
a limitless loss,

a winner only
when his pockets
were full
and his jokes were new.

Who was he now
at thirty-five –
a limited old man
who hadn't lived;
lingering on street corners,
searching for
shoot-the-breeze friendships
without commitments
or frontiers.

Rat-Like Dogs and Tattooed Men

(for Cathy Lafarge)

In Creepy Crawley
in West Sussex
big men with tattoos
walk rat-like dogs
into pubs.

When the rat-likes
go for the ankle bone
you are told
'Wouldn't touch you.'
Another says,
'He'd lick you to death.'

These big men,
one with his elbow
on his knee,
bellow down the ear
of your friend,

'He's a pisser,
pisses everywhere,
but I'll knock it
out of him,

a few round the head
and he'll sit up.'

You try not to look
at his tattoos
but you can't help it,
they're everywhere,
even on his lips.

'That one's a snake,'
he says,
'an anaconda
could eat elephant eggs
and spit out the shells,
could wrap himself
round the belly of an ass
and strangle it.'

Later, and glad to be home
the whole scene
dances in my head.

I question nothing
but the elephant eggs.

It's Platonic

Platonic my eye,

I yearn
for the fullness
of your tongue
making me
burst forth
pleasure after pleasure
after dark,

soaking all my dreams.

If You Want to Get Closer to God

A young one like you
shouldn't be left
on your own to wither,
not with the likes
of Kill Cassidy
knocking around.

He'd knock a son
out of you no problem,
no better man,
and he wouldn't even
work up a sweat.

Don't know what
the world's coming to
at all at all.
In Carraroe
they're swopping keys.

God will get
the upper hand yet,
they'll all end up
filling holes in the road
with their sins,
and their Jezebel shoes.

The Claddagh church
is my favourite
there's a lovely one
of the Virgin there
a right beauty,

they say the sculptor
hit ecstasy
before he finished
the five sorrows,

seven hours the ecstasy lasted
down on one knee, mouth open
chisel in the writing home position.

Badly off,
Bad-mouth Keogh
said it was no ecstasy
when he saw the bone setter
trotting on his jaw the next day.

Yeah, the Kill Cassidy's
the boy for you,
he'll knock a son all right
as many sons as you like
no better man,

I'm not mad about
the new Cathedral myself
too many frills for my liking,
keep it simple is my motto.
If you really want to get closer to God
Knock Shrine's your man,
no frills, no fuss
stark reality,
plenty of wheelchairs
plenty of buses.

New York

The Korean
who runs a flower shop
in Brooklyn says,

'Every day
people come in here
and steal from me.

They say,
when they are edging out
with my flower basket,

C'mon c'mon man
my wife just had four babies,
what can I tell you
I look at her
she gets pregnant.

Try taking this from me man
and for your trouble
I'll give you a bullet
in the head.

Although
all Koreans love a song,
I never say,
Have a nice day
I always say,
Take the flowers.'

H-Block Shuttle

(for L. McKeown)

We see nothing
from the Inter-Kesh-Shuttle
the H-mobile,
only the people seated
on the other side
(and no one really knows
what side they are on).

Somewhere between H's,
an overdue light bill,
thoughts of a holiday for two
(in anywhere but Gibraltar)
and the one who's doing life,

the H-mobile stops,
we wait for the doors to open
Tic toc, tic toc, tic toc.

Time for a head count.
He counts our heads
on his fingers
for a living,
while the people seated here
count the relatives
they have left
(some are running
out of uncles).
Some brazen it
with a false laugh,
some stare ahead
forgetting to blink.

A woman whispers
'We're going to the showers,'
others throw Mass card glances
at their shoes
(with them he counts
the back of their heads).

'Hey mister,
what do you do
for a shilling,
a queen's shilling?'

'I count heads
for a living,
my clean living.'

'Do you speak
to the heads
that you count?'

'I'm not paid
to speak to the heads
who don't count.

I'm paid to count
the heads who don't speak.'
'And why
do the heads
that you count
not speak?'

'Outside the dogs bark
to ensure
that the heads
who don't count
that I count
don't speak...'

'And what about
the no-windows scare?'

'No windows are there
to ensure
that the heads
who don't count
that I count
don't see.'

114

'And what is
it out there
that the heads
who you count
shouldn't see?'

'I count heads
on my fingers
for a living,
for my clean living,
for my queen's shilling.

I get paid
to count heads
who don't count,
not to tell you

what the heads
who don't count
that I count
shouldn't see.'

We see nothing
from the Inter-Kesh-Shuttle,
the H-mobile,
only the people seated
on the other side
(and no one really knows
what side they are on).

Trapped Doctor on Cork to Galway Bus

He was on the
Connemara run
for years,

twelve pins, twelve bins,
he knew them all.

He grew tired
of the mountains
and the sheep.

He longed
for the sight
of a field of grass,
nothing to write home about,
just a square field
an honest field
level and unpretentious.

He'd still take it
with a cow in it
maybe an old bath
a few rusty gates for a fence,
no sheep or mountains need apply.

He always said
there was a trapped doctor inside him
'One day I'll go back to college'
was his swan song.
Back to Cork
was as far as he got;
it's a long way
depending on how you walk it.

One day
on the Cork to Galway
on the hottest day of the year,
while we sizzled,
a draught fantasiser asked him,
could he open the door please.

He said it was against regulations.

That night
when he made love
to his wife,
he said,

'Gloria love, Gloria,
let on I'm tall.'

The Power of Prayer

I liked the way
my mother
got off her bike
to the side
while the bike
was still moving,
graceful as a bird.

We watched out for her
after Benediction.
It was a game –
who saw her head-scarf first,
I nearly always won.

The day the youngest
drank paraffin oil
we didn't know what to do.

All goofed round the gable end,
we watched, we waited,
head-scarf over the hill.

Knowing there was something wrong
she threw the bike down
and ran.

She cleared fences
with the ailing child,
Mrs Burke gave a spoon of jam,
the child was saved.
Marched indoors
we feared the worst,
our mother knew
what the problem was.

'Not enough prayers
are being said in this house.'

While the paraffin child
bounced in her cot
we prayed and prayed.

We did the Creed,
a blast of the Beatitudes
the black fast was mentioned,
the Confiteor was said
like it was never said before,
Marie Goretti was called
so was Martha,
we climaxed on the Magnificat.
After that it was all personal stuff.

I liked the way
my mother
got off her bike
to the side
while the bike
was still moving,
graceful as a bird.

For good neighbours with jam
for Pope's intentions
for God's holy will
for the something of saints
the forgiveness of sins
for the conversion of Russia
for Doctor Noel Browne
for the lads in the Congo
for everyone in Biafra
for Uncle Andy's crazy bowel
for ingrown toenails
and above all
for the grace of a happy death.

Jackdaw Jaundice

When the geezer
on the bridge
near Heuston Station
asked the nun
for the price
of a cup of tea,

her answer was in
the hooves from hell sounds
she made with her heels.

He replied in winegorian chant,

'Typical jackdaw jaundice,
clip-clopitty-clop
and a black sail away.'

I Want to Make Love to Kim Basinger

I'm terrified
of hairdressers
who always say
Are you going
to the dance
tonight love?

I always say yes
even though
I'm never going
to the dance
tonight love.

They say the dance
I say the dance
we all say the dance
we say, the dance.

They think
I should be going
to the dance
and what they think goes.

I always
have my hair done
so I can look good
in the bath
in case
Kim Basinger
calls round.

If she takes the trouble
to climb four flights,
the lift isn't there
so it doesn't work,
and if she takes

the further trouble
of five lefts,
two rights
and three straight aheads,
I want to be ready for her.

I never told them this
at the hairdressers,
I always say dance dance,
I'm going to the dance.

It pleases them,
they go from there
they spread the web
cast the nets
they get to the root,
before I know it
I'm on the Persian carpet.

One called Consumpta consumes,
she talks in scrunch and blow dry
kiss curl mousse or gel
bee-hive-jive, French plait
Afro comb all alone.

With her, everyone is my woman;
my woman this, my woman that
my woman with the highlights
my woman with the perm
my woman with the worm.

When consuming Consumpta says
did you just have a baby,
your hair is falling
into your tea.
I always say yes
I start to shout,
I say yes Consumpta yes.

Give her anything
but split ends.

She says,
give me anything
but split ends.

No split ender
ever shifted
the bull of the ball
and we do want
the bull of the ball
don't we
otherwise why bother
getting our hair done
in the first place,
then she says Spanish,
she says Comprendo.
I say yes Consumpta yes.
Once after shouting
over her shoulder
to other, as yet,
less Consuming Consumptas;
Remind me I owe the till three pounds,
she looked me in the eye,
through the mirror,
and said,

hot oil that's it,
hot oil
is the jigger you need.
Steeped in it
for twenty
you'll come out
a new woman,
you'll taste your tea then
and it won't be wearing a moustache,
mark my words.

And dance, dance
don't talk to me
about dance,
you'll be dancing
that much,
they'll be seeing
sparks off your nipples,

hot oil, that's it
the jigger you need,

hot oil today
the bull of the ball tonight.
Mark my words.

FROM **HIGHER PURCHASE**
(1996)

The Flogger

A man with such a belly
can never ever become a flogger
KAFKA: The Trial

He wanted to be a flogger –
not just any old
swing the taws
Tom-Jack run-o'-the-mill flogger
he wanted to be
the best flogger in town.

His father, a fines administrator
his mother, a fine administrator's wife
he knew about the letter of the law.

He longed to flog.
He would flog miserable souls
to within an inch of their miserable lives.

He fancied they would go away galled –
but confident that they were flogged,
not by any Jack-Tom chancer flogger.

They would respond to
how's she cutting greetings,
'flogged' they'd say,
'not by any run-o'-the-chancer flogger
by the foulest flogger in town,
and furthermore it was a Double
Special Offer Monday flogging
me and the wife together
Me with the left hand
the wife with the right hand
our agonies complete.'

When the town flogger
sullied his career
by blind dating a one-time flogged soul,
the fines administrator's son
took the reins.

The slim back
was his favourite
the back to tear a shirt from
the cat-o'-nines-delight.

But this flogger,
not just any
swing the mill
run-Jack-over-Tom flogger
was a very fair flogger.

He always gave the choice
'take it off or have it torn off,'
that won him acclaim
that, and his Special Offer Mondays.

Like every good flogger
he had his faults,
he had five stomachs
he had to keep them filled
he dipped often into other people's pots.

Eventually he got caught,
his father, a fines administrator
his mother, a fine administrator's wife.
The flogger, the fair old flogger
the 'take it off or have it torn off' flogger
got fifty lashes
inferior lashes by his standards,
the shame of the flogger
being flogged left its mark,
especially when he met
souls he had flogged
and flogged well,
his shame left him smaller
and red all over.

He Could Get Radio Prague

When he said
he could get
an oil rig for scrap
just like that,

and that
he could get
Radio Prague
on his transistor,

and that
he never backed horses
each way or in a placepot
only on the nose
always on the nose,

and that
he knew rakes of really famous actors
because of all the films
he was extra in,

and that
he was only hangin' round here
until Peter, their Peter,
came over from Canada with the jingle,

and that
it wouldn't bother him one bit
if he never saw
this fuck arse of a town ever again,

no one at the bus stop anythinged him.

He Is Not Thinking About Last Night

He is sitting
on a bollard
his head in his hands –
rats and ladders
from liqui-land
hoping for
a lift to town.

Cars are passing him goodo.
He is thinking into his hands
'How am I going to get a lift to town
for the cure, Jesus Mercy Mary help.'

He wasn't even out last night
he was in with M spirit Esquire
gut rotter
cell begrudger
brain emptier
usher to oblivion.

He head-in-the-handed it so long
there was talk of a plaque,
mind you it was only small talk.

The dissenters say he dogged it
and no plaque should he get,
they said he should be plaqueless.

They had a main speaker
who shouted from the back
of a rejuvenated Hillman Imp.
At times they joined in.

Usually the main speaker let rip
'Plaque what plaque, plaque my eye,
did they give me a plaque
when I got cancer of the ear lobe
and my ear fell off,

not on your ninny,
cop yourself ons they gave me
and plenty of them.

Haven't you got another ear they shouted
listen more carefully
with the one you've got
and you might be better off,
some things aren't worth hearing
some things are better left unsaid
that's the type of plaque I got.'

In time the plaque went up
and as plaques go this one didn't
weather beaten it stayed like himself
long after hours and hours.

Still the cars never stopped
but they slowed to a crawl.
Usually the eldest would do the honours
unless the eldest was insane
or under the throes of botulism,
then it would fall to the second eldest.

Males had superiority on Sundays,
Tuesdays and every third Saturday
all other days females read first,
except when the interlopers
tried to get a piece of the action.

Then the townies
even the dissenters
would take on plaque pride.

A deep breath was taken first;
these are the very boyos
who said earlier
'plaque what plaque, plaque my eye',

now they are telling the interlopers
'if any plaque needs readin' aloud
in this town

we have the vehicles
and the voice power
so feck off to Loughrea, Lockjaw
or Monaghan town for yourselves'.

So this day, a Sunday,
the plaque was read
the vehicle, a rejuvenated Hillman Imp
the occupant, a show-off
wearing one ear and beaming
with plaque pride
(the interlopers were balking in the bushes),

'This man is not thinking about last night
night of passion how good it wasn't,
he is hoping one of you family albums
with the lattice vests
the gaudy shades
the tattoos,
will stop your tripod philosophies
your umbrella loins
your barium meals
your poxy cars
and give him a lift to town
for the cure Jesus Mercy Mary help,

before his
soap-box eyes
challenge onto his palms
tour guide up his sleeves
slip-jig round his wind pipe
hammer down the town without him and jive.'

Donna Laura

Petrarch you louser,
I'm here plagued with the plague
and you're off chasing
scab free thighs.

Milli is the only one
who stood by me,
not that you could say stood,
she blesses herself
a thousand times a day
her head always ground-ward bound
prayers and half prayers
tripping her as she goes.

She scalds the arse off me
with the hot bricks
she keeps pushing between the sheets.

Between the shivers
the high fevers
and the hot bricks
I'm beside myself with anxiety.

Francesco, remember that Good Friday
in the church of Santa Chiara?
You nearly knocked a column
gazing at me
plague free at the time
I had hardly a pimple.

*Milli, off your knees,
and fetch me that ointment and gauze
wet my lips while you're at it.*

It was Easter before
we met again
those three days
like three lifetimes,

little did I know
that the sonnets
were oozing out of you
and little Madonna Laura
was sparking them off.

Milli don't forget
to wrap a clean rag
around my chin when I go
give up that snivelling
and keep them Aves to yourself.

Whenever there was
a whiff of Pope in the background
you no longer saw me
only chalices, gold embroidered cloaks
large tracts of land
and Bulls, loads of Papal Bulls.

O Petrarch, you poser,
you were always swaggering
in and out of the Papal courts.

As for the sonnets
you were seen tearing them up
and throwing them petal-like
around the marketplace,
the Pope thought your piss was lemonade.

Petrarch, may you get what I have,
whoever rolled back that stone
should have rolled it over your head.

Higher Purchase

We saw them take
her furniture out,

the new stuff
her kids boasted about
six months before.

The Chesterfield Suite
the pine table and chairs
the posh lamp
the phone table,
though they had no phone.

When it was going in
we watched with envy
she told her kids out loud
'You're as good as anyone else
on this street'.

When it was coming out
no one said anything,
only one young skut
who knew no better, shouted,

'Where will ye put the phone now,
when it comes.'

When the Big Boys Pulled Out

In S.P.S.
we parted the nuts
we parted the washers
between this and lunch time
we smoked.

A nut in this barrel
a washer in that barrel
never a washer in with a nut
never a nut with a washer be.

After lunch
was much the same,
divide and conquer
nut and washer
no thought for cancer
we all smoked on.

We had plenty of
nut and washer jokes
but they were all played out
and only used
when a new girl started.

We were cruel
sending her for a glass hammer,
a bucket of compressed air.
Soon enough she was flashing the ash,
and goading us on an all-out strike,
when we got dermatitis.

This decisive thinker won us over
in a hurry, making her part
of our nut and washer brigade.

Our fag breaks
became our summer holidays
when the Big Boys pulled out.

Now everything
was in the one barrel
butts, nuts, bolts,
washers, dryers
eye shadows
wedding dresses
bell-bottoms
hopes, dreams, fantasies
platforms,
Beatlemania,

Costa del Sols
where-will-you-get-work-now jokes
that were no jokes
Benidorums
all alore-ums.

Our fag breaks
became our summer holidays
when the Big Boys pulled out.
No further need
of our discretion
a nut here
a washer there.

The Flute Girl's Dialogue

Plato, come out now
with your sunburnt legs on ya
don't tell me to play to myself
or to the other women.

'Discourse in Praise of Love' indeed.

Bad mannered lot,
even if I cough when I come into the room
it does not stop your bleating.
That couch over there seats two comfortably
yet every time I enter
there's four of you on it
acting the maggot
then if Socrates walks in,
the way you all suck up to him.

Small wonder Plato
you have a leg to stand on
after all the red herrings
you put in people's mouths.
You hide behind Eryximachus
and suspend me like tired tattle.

'Tell the Flute Girl to go' indeed.

Let me tell you Big Sandals
the Flute Girl's had it.
When I get the sisters in here
we are going to sit on the lot of you,
come out then gushing platonic.

The Flute Girl knows
the fall of toga tune
the flick of tongue
salt-dip hemlock-sip
eye to the sky tune

hand on the thigh tune
moan and whimper talk
dual distemper talk.

When you played I listened,
when I play, prick up your ears.

The Trouble With Karen Reilly

She is mirror mirror
she is too much eye-liner
she is lipstick redder than blood
she is Jon Bon Jovi
she is the salt.

Her skirt's
way too short
her jumper's
way too low
and cheek
she could fire it
faster than lead.

If anyone called
she was ready,
she was always ready
set and she went
for spills and thrills

down the Falls
in a stolen car
a back seat passenger
with non-stop gossip
of the weekend disco
who shifted who
who got the ride

she laughed for nothing
she sang for a hoot
'Everything I do
I do it for you.'

She was wild
she was free
she was Bon Jovi,

with the bullet in her back
she was Clegged.

Mothercare

The girls came over
to see the new buggy,
the rainbow buggy,
the sunshine stripes.

O.K. it was expensive
but it was the best
and welfare pitched in.

It had everything –
she listed its finer points,
underbelly things we hadn't seen.

A little touch here
and it collapses
a little touch there
and it's up like a shot,
you barely touch this –
and you're in another street
another town.

A mind of its own
a body like a rocket
it's yours to control –
just like that.

She swears she'll keep it well
immaculate, she says, immaculate.

When she's nearly eighteen
it will still be new,
Tomma-Lee will be two and a half,

she can sell it then
and fetch a high price,

almost as much as she paid.

The Quarrel

Zeus, loveen,
help me, help my son
who runs rings around me,
but not for long.

That rotten cur Agamemnon
has stolen his prize
and you know the way
our family gets about prizes.

Remember that time
we won the two turkeys at bingo,
they all said it was a fix
and I threatened to bring up
every last crab from the deep
to piss on their cabbage.

And you, you know all,
must know how I have defended you
against that Shantalla crowd
who call you The Bonking Swan
behind your lovely back.

Bow your head,
loving know all,
let everyone see the sign.
Show them die-hards
my invitation
didn't say don't come.

When Zeus bowed
his holy head
the heavens shook,
swans all over Sligo
were taking oaths
and cover, much cover.

Hera wasn't one bit pleased
'I see slithery feet was here,
begging as usual,

what did she want this time –
to plait your sable brows?'

Zeus tried to interrupt.

'Didn't I see her
with my own ox-eye
wrapped around your knees.

Fine thing
in my own house.
I can't glide into the kitchen
and have a cup of tea
and a kit-kat
but old slithery feet
has my tiles ruined,
well I'm fed up with it, by jingo.'

Just then Hephaestus appeared,
sick as a gone-off mackerel
that the dinner would be spoiled
with all the quarrelling.
(Zeus nipped out for a solpadeine)
'Mother,' he said
'never mind that Barry's tea
drink this and swallow your resentments
you can't win against Zeus.

One time for nothing
he caught me by the foot
and hurled me into
the middle of next year
I'm still dizzy and lame.'

Hera laughed at this.
Apollo, mad to get
on *The Late Late Show*,
took out his harp, by Jove,
and they all drank nectar
till the bulls came home
and the craic was mighty
and Hera forgetting her jingo
let Thetis slide easy into the sea.

Whiplashed

My client, your honour,
is experiencing great difficulty
sitting from a standing position
and standing from a sitting position.

His pelvic spring
is not what it used to be,
in fact on the night in question
his pelvic spring sprung.

His left trapezius muscle is trapped
and is starting to make encores
half two degrees south of his right hippus,
this carry-on is involuntary.

Any examination of the throacic spine
activates the voice box,
and my client keeps repeating
in a sirloin staccato,

Your numbskull killed a swan
with my new numberella.

Since the whiplash
my client is left-handed.
This makes shoe removing very difficult,
especially if you're in Dublin
and your shoes are in Cork.

Another thing, your honour,
since the lash
my client is unable to –
how shall we put it – flatuate.
This unfortunate condition
is causing a false fullness
which my client erogenously believes
will only be relieved
by forty lumber punctures.

Have you any idea, your honour,
the cost of a lumber puncture nowadays?

I implore your honour,
in your decision for compensation,

to think long and hard
about pelvic springing
which is still negative
despite 140 calls to
Orgasmic Orla
on the 'Let's Talk Dirty' line.

My client reminds me, your honour,
that before this pelvic punishment,
he was cock of the walk.

Remapping the Borders

In Texas
after the conference
they put on a céilí,
nearly everyone danced,
a few of us Margarita'd.

In jig time
everyone knew everyone.
After the Siege of Ennis
a woman asked me,
'Could you see my stocking belt
as I did the swing?'

I was taken aback.

Me, thigh, knee, no,
I saw nothing.
I saw no knee
no luscious thigh
no slither belt,
with lace embroidered border
that was hardly a border at all.

I was looking for the worm in my glass.

I thought about her after,
when I was high above St Louis.
I'm glad I didn't see
her silk white thighs
her red satin suspender belt
with black embroidered border
that was hardly a border at all.

I swear to you
I saw nothing,
not even the worm
lying on his back
waiting to penetrate my tongue.

Mamorexia

You should be
down on your knees
thanking God
with the lovely
husband ya have.

Look at Beatrice Cohen
the teeth nearly rotten
in her head –
what chance has she?

And her sister
spitting out babies
every time she coughs
and none of them
havin' any fathers,
except that lad
with the dark skin.

She was told often enough
no good would come of her
swanking round the docks
in those sling backs.

Lookit you
with those two angels
with them lovely
white bobby socks on them
and their father's eyes.

Cop yourself on –
your shadow looks
better than ya,
pull yourself together
and for crying out loud
go and eat something

something decent.

The Winner

It was his dog
you could tell the way
it clung round his neck
like a collar.

The remote control was his
his name was etched
with a broken penknife
across the top – His.

He always got
the biggest chop
when he was eating,
the biggest chop
he said, down boy down.

He spent all day every
burping and channel surfing
with his own ensignified remote control.

He was in Minnesota once
to check the time.
He always said,
'When I was in Minnesota
the chops were much bigger.'
He said it every day
chops, Minnesota, bigger.

His wife wished
and wished
that he would
go to Minnesota
and stick to
the biggest chop
and check the time.

He wasn't into divorce
or dirty dish washing,
he stayed and stayed
with his dog collar
his remote control
his greasy chop.

Got to hand it to him
on that remote control
he was fast,
he couldn't be beaten
he channel surfed all day,

at night he always came first.

The Taxi Man Knows

I see them going off there
and hardly a stitch on them
one young thing
I swear to God
you could see her cheeks
another lassie
you could see her tonsils

and they come home then
crying over spilt milk

if she was my daughter
I'd give her something to cry over.

When it Comes to the Crutch

Most of Joy-Roy-Gang
end up on crutches,
some die all of a sudden
some die all of the time
others join the Joy-Roy-Groupies Club,
they have afternoon crutch races.
Better than snatching
where the buzz is only part-time.

Hard chaws anyway
(look at Elvis Kelly
got a hook caught in his flesh
nearly lost his primer).
If you're on crutches
you're doubly hard.
So it is written on the fag wall:
Two legs good
Two legs with sticks gooder.

At the crutch race
this guy is hot, shit hot
hops like a pro, a real pro
he nearly always wins,
he jibes the others,

'Sissies, step-in-the-hallas
couldn't catch a wan-winged butterfly
with asthma, ye pussies.'

They know he's getting
too big for his boots
they all think it –
leaning against the fag wall.

The head crutcher,
(a right heel)
is losing face
he tells the asthma joker,

'You break
one of my crutches
I'll break
two of your legs'.

The leaners laugh last.

Gretta's Hex

For years
Gretta cleaned
the factory
down the road from us.

When she had to have
her dog put down
because he had the mange

she got the runs
for three days.
Babbs Laffey
told the whole street.

Before this
she never missed work
not when her four girls
had the measles,
nor when the Pope came
to Ballybrit.

Now she went to the boss
she asked him for time off
to mourn her dead dog
she had long before the four girls
who recovered well from measles.

The boss said,
'Sorry Ann
I mean Gretta
1 can't spare you now
what with Sadie,
I mean Annie, on holiday
and the two Marys out sick,

you're the only one here
who can operate that buffer.

Can't you mourn your dead dog here,
take an extra fifteen minutes
at tea break, good girl'.

All these foul noises
from the boss's mouth
upset Gretta
who never missed
a cleaning factory
four girls with measles
young people of Ireland
Pope filled Ballybrit day
in her life.

From her grief stricken
dead dog hole in the heart
she wished him:

Sightreducingweekendsahead
buffer festering
the company of bats
the company of bees (over-tired and hungry ones)
nouns with genitive singular inflection

verbs with janitor holding injections
slow dipping in the wallet (by others)
Sadie and the two Marys
and above all
sleepus interruptus with demonos oftenus
plus an extra fifteen minutes in hell.
Amen.

Prism

After the man
up our street
stuck broken glass
on top of his back wall
to keep out
those youngsters
who never stopped
teasing his
Doberman Pinscher,

he put
the safety chain
on the door,
sat at the kitchen window,
let out a nervous laugh
and watched
the Castle Park sun
divide the light
and scatter it
all over his property.

The Temptation of Phillida

When she was younger
much younger
she liked to look deep
into men's eyes.
A friend told her
men can make you come
with their eyes.

One day at the traffic lights
she saw eyes
she wanted to fall into.

The owner of these baby blues
was leaning against the jewellery shop window
sucking a woodbine.
She kept looking deeper and deeper
she could see sapphires, rubies, white gold.
Eternity rings, paternity rings
gold rings gold things
every conceivable carat
heart in hand rings
heart in bag rings
heart in honey rings
O honey.

'Do you fuck?' said the woodbine.

'Only men with big crocodiles,' she said.

He threw the butt down and walked away.

She called after him,

'Is your crocodile
finger licking good
or index finger big?'

He started to run.

Spiked

On the way to court
they did the caterpillar crawl,
all hitting the same stride
jumpers hanging
long beyond the fingers.

They quarter-filled the court
'Grievous Bodily Harm'
was up again
this time it wasn't too bad
only assault with menaces
and a wheel brace.

The caterpillar crew hooted
when he back-cheeked the judge,
the judge warned
and warned again.

When the court adjourned for lunch
they sat in the long hall
on the back of seats
walkmans, talkmans,
gum gobblers,

Maria who and Kelly what,
Jimmy and Sonia
always a Sonia
praising their idol to the skies,

the leather jacket cut of him
how he sorted that judge
how he turned round
and gave the fist
bare faced
fearing nothing and no one.

More smoke
rings were made
butts were flicked in the air
a thousand curses

court was back in session.
'Grievous' made more jestures
finger and fist
and fist again.

The pillar crew were roused
they whistled
through their fingers
in unison
no calming them now,

'cept when the judge
passed sentence
giving 'Grievous'
four of the best
to be served on Spike.

Lower lips
were dropping
eyes were welling
mascara was getting smeared.
A girl with a spiral perm
addressed the court,

'I'll write
every day Grevie,
promise you will too.'

'Sure babe, why wouldn't I?'

He made a fist
with the free hand
he boxed the air
they cheered
he made a fist again,

soon the free hand
was cuffed
no more fist in the air
he gave them the chin.

They knew what he meant.

Night Noon and Nora

He was dead
no two ways about it
only his bones
never hit the clay
they were home
hitting the roof
when visitors came
he didn't want company
he only wanted her
not to leave him
to his thoughts
and his tea-stained eyes.

Master of mime,
he put on fantasy stockings
he sat on fantasy chairs
he called her
night noon and Nora,
the woman he nearly married
forty years ago
the woman whose husband Pious
got back cancer
from carrying her troubles.

He went for a spoon
and he brought back a fish.
Once at Eyre Square, he cried,
'I don't know who I am
promise you'll never leave me Nora
even when I'm asleep.'

Her word was gospel,
she got tired nodding
but she never slept,
except for the forty winks last September.
She remembered every wink
like thick soup, she said.

She went to grief councillors,
she told them
bones in the house
spirit in the sky
stockings that aren't there
chairs that are no chairs
fish that are spoons
he's calling me Nora
I'm Bridget on the brink of a breakdown
help me.

They told her to let go
and let ever loving God
do night watchman.

The last straw was when
he turned up at second Mass
wearing only a lost look,
his clothes were at home
on the back of a chair,
a real chair.

She screamed out
to her ever loving God,
'I'm Bridget on the brink of a breakdown,
deliver me.'

God wasn't in at the time
he was down in Middle street
making mince meat out of Pious's cancer,
everyone knew that.